REAL WORLD ECONOMICS™

How a
Depression
Works

Jason Porterfield

+6.73
+1.33

+21.64
+14.83
+3.24
+9.19
+32.47
+11.02
+2.35
+25.05
+2.42
+5.53
+13.41

ROSEN
PUBLISHING®

New York

Published in 2010 by The Rosen Publishing Group, Inc.
29 East 21st Street, New York, NY 10010

Library of Congress Cataloging-in-Publication Data

Porterfield, Jason.
How a depression works / Jason Porterfield.—1st ed.
     p. cm.—(Real world economics)
Includes bibliographical references and index.
ISBN-13: 978-1-4358-5322-5 (library binding)
1. Depressions—Juvenile literature. 2. Business cycles—Juvenile literature.
3. Business forecast—Juvenile literature. I. Title.
HB3716.P67 2009
338.5'42—dc22

                                                                        2008049265

Manufactured in the United States of America

CPSIA Compliance Information: Batch #BR902021YA: For further information contact Windmill Books, New York, New York at
1-866-478-0556.

On the cover: Traders on the floor of the New York Stock Exchange react with anxiety to plummeting stock prices in 2008. The U.S. economy entered a recession in 2008, the worst downturn since the Great Depression of the 1920s and 1930s. Many economists thought that the bottom had not yet been reached. Some even feared that the country—and the world— might enter another depression.

Contents

INTRODUCTION

In the second half of 2008, every new day seemed to bring more bad economic news. People were losing their jobs, and fewer of them were able to find new work. At the same time, prices were increasing for food, gas, and other goods. Many people who borrowed money to buy a home or other large purchases in earlier years when cash and credit were flowing freely were now struggling to pay their home mortgages and other debts. Some were losing their homes. Even some banks, unable to collect on the loans they had issued, were having trouble staying open. Because of this economic turmoil, many people had to make changes in how they spent their money. These decisions affected everything from the kind of clothes they bought and where they bought them to how much they drove and in what kind of car. Families skipped vacations or cut back on movies and restaurant meals.

When the economy struggles, experts try to explain why these changes occur. They see the ups and downs of the

economy as part of a continuous cycle of ups and downs. These trends and cycles belong to the extraordinarily complex field of economics. Economics is the study of the way money, goods, and services are made, distributed, and bought.

National economies can go through many different stages as they react to changing conditions. For example, inflation is the general increase in the cost of goods and services for the average person. Bubbles occur when part of the economy appears healthier than it really is, while booms are the rapid growth of parts of the economy. A relatively new phenomenon called globalization refers to the interconnection of businesses and industries around the world. Recessions are usually brief economic downturns that occur when the value of a nation's goods and services declines. It often takes several months or even a couple of years for an economy to come out of a recession. The end of a recession is usually signaled by rising employment levels and greater spending by consumers.

If a recession lasts a very long time and keeps getting worse, it could turn into a depression. Depressions are recessions marked by very sharp, severe drops in business activity, employment, and the stock market. While economies usually come out of recessions within a year or two, depressions can last much longer.

Depressions also affect a broader range of people than a recession does. A large percentage of the population struggles with economic hardship and inflation. The most recent economic depression in the United States was the Great Depression, which lasted from 1929 through the 1930s and affected people and nations throughout the world. While the United States eventually came out of the Great Depression, the memory of hard times lasted for decades and helped reshape the country's economic policies and institutions, many of which are still in place today.

CHAPTER ONE

THE THEORY BEHIND DEPRESSIONS

The economy of the United States is always changing. Different aspects of the economy, such as employment, wages, and output, are in a constant state of flux—either improving or worsening, going up or going down. The economy may go through a period of incredible growth for a year or two before leveling off. The economy may stagnate, or remain relatively unchanged, and then be followed by another period of growth. It may even fall into a recession or depression. Recessions happen when the economy slows for a period of time because fewer people are buying goods and services, and fewer people have jobs. This results in companies producing fewer goods and offering even fewer jobs. Extremely long or severe recessions are called depressions.

Recessions often mean hard times for many people. Prices may go down but so, too, does the actual value of money. There are fewer jobs because companies aren't hiring or are even laying off their workers. The stock market declines sharply (which means the value of many companies' stocks falls).

These things remain true during a depression, though to a more extreme degree.

A depression is a rare but extreme form of recession. Depressions are marked by a major and long-lasting shortfall

Many people do less shopping and cut back on spending during an economic downturn. Businesses may be forced to close if their customers stop spending.

in consumers' ability to buy goods and services, compared with the economy's potential ability to produce them. During a depression, unemployment may increase dramatically. Lenders stop offering people credit (the ability to obtain cash or buy things on the promise of repayment in the future). Fewer people invest their money in the stock market, and the value of money itself goes down. Prices fall as demand for goods evaporates. People's assets, such as their homes, lose value. Less buying and selling takes place and bankruptcies rise.

The economy becomes stuck in this cycle because vast numbers of people—many of them unemployed, working for less than they used to, or worried about losing their jobs—can't afford goods and services. At the same time, companies aren't hiring people because they aren't making any money when their products are going unsold. It often takes years and dramatic change sparked by the government or outside events for an economy to climb out of a depression. Government intervention in a depressed economy can include large public spending and building projects, cash "bailouts" of struggling industries, the setting of lower interest rates to make loans cheaper, and taxpayer relief in the form of tax cuts or rebates.

People wait in line at an unemployment office in Rhode Island. Unemployment benefits provide a safety net for workers who lose their jobs.

Economic Indicators

The words "depression" and "recession" both describe economic downturns. Generally, recessions that are very severe or last for a very long time are considered depressions. It isn't always clear how they are different. For example, until the Great Depression of the 1930s, any downturn in the United States economy was called a depression. At that time, economists came up with the word "recession" to describe less severe downturns than the one the United States was experiencing.

Today, experts use statistics and data called economic indicators to judge the economy's performance. Economic indicators reflect how well certain parts of the economy are performing. The unemployment rate is one such number. The unemployment rate measures the number of people who do not have jobs but are looking for work. A low unemployment rate shows that companies are doing well and hiring workers.

A rising unemployment rate often means that some companies are shedding workers while others are simply not hiring. This can be a strong sign that the economy is weakening.

Inflation refers to the rising cost of goods and services over a period of time. It can also mean the decreasing value of money. In both cases, goods and services become more expensive, either because their sticker prices are rising or because your dollar is worth less than it used to be. It buys less than it did before the inflationary period began. During a period of inflation, it takes more money to buy things than it did before. Economists generally agree that inflation happens when the money supply grows faster than the economy grows. There is too much money in circulation in the economy (perhaps due to easy loans and credit, and rising wages) and not enough production of goods and services. So, demand is high, supply is low, and prices rise. When there is a lot of money in circulation, its value—its actual purchasing power—decreases.

Two of the most important economic indicators are numbers called the gross national product and the gross domestic product. The gross national product (GNP) is the market value of all final goods and services made using resources owned by people of that economy. These resources can include materials, stores, or factories that are located in other countries. So, an American-based company that sells clothing in France made from Chinese silk and manufactured in Indian factories contributes to the GNP of the United States. The GNP of the United States can include cars or other factory goods produced by American companies in other parts of the world.

The gross domestic product (GDP) represents a part of the GNP. It stands for the total value of all final goods and services at current market prices produced within an economy within a given year. In this case, the goods and services must be produced on American soil.

Both the GDP and the GNP are important numbers for economists because they reflect the health of the economy. If these numbers go up over a period of time, it means that the economy is generally strong. If their rate of increase slows, it shows that the growth of the economy itself is slowing, and there may be trouble on the way. A drop in these numbers could signal the beginning of a recession. If the GDP drops by more than 10 percent, it signals the beginning of a depression.

The Business Cycle

Economists explain the ups and downs of the economy as simply being a part of the business cycle. Business cycles are made up of four phases: peak, recession, trough, and recovery. Economists cannot predict the exact phases of a cycle or say how long they may last. However, the economy is always in one of these four phases. When shown on a graph, these phases look like a roller coaster. The cycle begins with a peak. It drops with a recession. When it hits the trough, it starts climbing again as it recovers. It reaches another peak, and the cycle starts again.

Peaks occur when the economy is performing near its highest possible level. Economists use economic indicators to figure out whether the economy is trending upward or downward. Economists consider the economy strong if unemployment is low and the GDP is rising. In a peak, the GDP has reached its maximum.

The peak ends when the economy starts to contract, or shrink. The economy enters a recession at this point. A recession is a downturn in the business cycle. The GDP declines

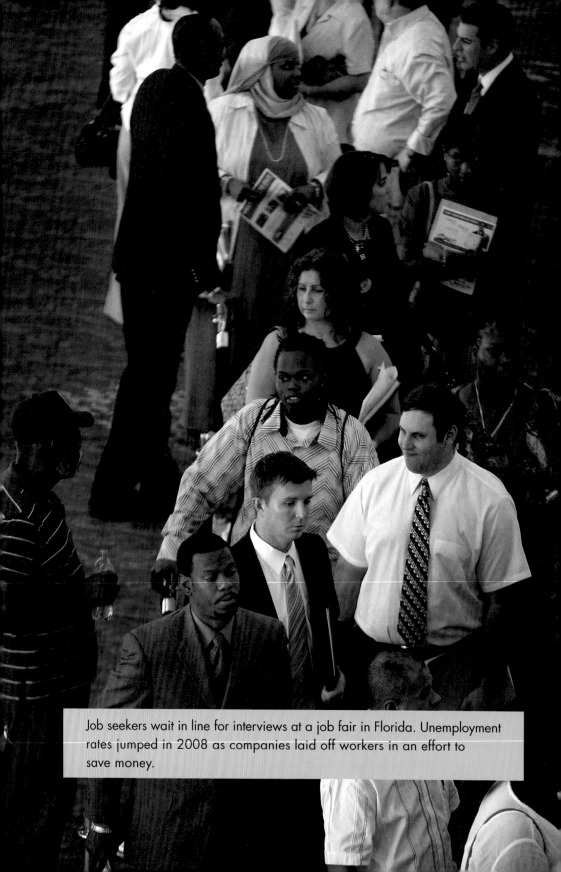

Job seekers wait in line for interviews at a job fair in Florida. Unemployment rates jumped in 2008 as companies laid off workers in an effort to save money.

during a recession. Corporate profits may also go down. At the same time, unemployment may go up, as fewer people looking for work are able to find jobs. In the most extreme cases, recessions become depressions.

Ultimately, the economy will reach a point where unemployment stops increasing and economic output stops decreasing. This point is the trough, the third stage of the business cycle. The trough is the bottom of the business cycle. The length of time between the peak and the trough marks how long the recession has lasted. The trough represents both good and bad news for the economy. On one hand, it is the lowest point in the business cycle and represents its worst conditions. At the same time, it also marks the beginning of the last phase of the business cycle, the recovery period.

During the recovery period, the economy once again begins growing, sometimes vigorously. Companies start hiring again, and people begin spending more money. Production is increased to meet this rising demand, resulting in more hiring and more consumer spending. A positive cycle begins and gathers momentum. The economy may even enter a boom period, in which it grows very rapidly. The economy begins working its way to another peak, at which point the business cycle starts over and again begins its inevitable move downward.

Early Depressions

The last major economic depression to hit the United States began in the late-1920s and ended in the mid-1940s. The economy has not come close to such a major economic collapse since. However, during the nineteenth century, recessions and even depressions were quite common.

Often, depressions would be set off by a panic of some kind. Banks might suddenly discover that they had overextended credit and could not collect the money owed them. As a result, they'd be forced to close. Or, stock traders might manipulate the market by offering useless stocks or properties at high prices. Once the real value of these items became apparent, prices would collapse and people would lose fortunes. A ripple effect of plummeting stock prices and investor panic would spread throughout the economy, damaging even previously healthy companies. During this period, the government did very little to regulate the economy, and bank and stock market misman-agement and panics were relatively common.

During the nineteenth century, five major financial panics hit the United States: in 1819, 1837, 1857, 1873, and 1893. All five led to depressions. The Panic of 1819 resulted in the first depression in U.S. history. The economy had been strug-gling since the United States went to war with Great Britain in the War of 1812 (1812–1814). At the time, cotton was one of the country's biggest exports and a key part of the economy. Cotton prices fell sharply in 1819. At the same time, credit froze, and banks and lenders were forced to call in loans. Farms were foreclosed (taken over by the banks that farmers owed money to), and many banks collapsed during the panic. The panic lasted until 1821.

Several factors caused the Panic of 1837. Cotton prices had again collapsed. Wheat crops had failed. Land speculation (in which people rapidly purchased and sold overvalued land in the hope of making a profit) resulted in a burst real estate bubble and the loss of investments. The variety of currency circulating in the United States (at the time, many states issued their own currency) caused confusion and inflation. Financial problems

Farm workers pick cotton in Mississippi during the depression of the 1890s, which was the country's worst depression until the Great Depression began in 1929.

in Great Britain had ripple effects in the United States. The depression that resulted from all of these stresses was the second-longest in the country's history, lasting for about six years. Many financial firms in New York City and state-sponsored banks failed, and the cost of labor dropped sharply. Real estate and food prices also dropped. Land speculators who had bought acreage at high prices were wiped out, as were farmers and planters who couldn't get decent prices for their crops.

The Panic of 1857, in contrast, was triggered by a single event—the collapse of the Ohio Life Insurance and Trust Company. The company, which mostly operated out of New York City, had overspeculated on railroads before collapsing. Stock prices of other companies plummeted when the company collapsed. More than nine hundred investment firms failed because of the panic. The economy didn't begin recovering until 1859.

Railroad speculation also set off the Panic of 1873. The investment firm Jay Cooke and Company collapsed, causing the stock market to drop and many businesses to fail. About three million American workers lost their jobs because of the panic. Food prices fell sharply. Many farmers once again couldn't get good prices for their crops, causing widespread poverty in farming communities. The depression lasted for five years, ending in 1878.

The Panic of 1893 was the last depression to hit the country during the nineteenth century. It was also the worst in the country's history until the Great Depression. The stock market dropped that spring and then crashed in June, as panicked stockholders sold off their shares. By the end of the year, more than sixteen thousand businesses had failed. Among the failed businesses were 153 railroads and nearly 500 banks. Unemployment climbed until one in six Americans was unemployed. The depression finally ended in 1897.

Ten Great Questions
to Ask a Financial Adviser

1. How do depressions begin?

2. How long can a depression last?

3. How can I protect my savings and investments during a depression?

4. How do I know that a depression has ended?

5. Why don't more recessions turn into depressions?

6. What laws and regulations protect the economy from a depression?

7. Who decides that a depression has begun or ended?

8. Will another depression happen in the United States?

9. How is the U.S. economy linked to the economies of other countries?

10. How do financial recoveries begin?

CHAPTER TWO

HOW DEPRESSIONS START

It often seems as if economic depressions are set off by a single event. The stock market fails, and many investors lose money. A major industry may collapse and suddenly put thousands of people out of work. The beginning of a depression may be marked by bank failures or a sudden tightening of credit. While these dramatic events may appear to be the cause, they often follow other economic troubles that may have been brewing for months or even years before the depression hits.

The Causes of Depressions

Prices for goods and services rise and fall over time. Economists call these changes "fluctuations." Local fluctuations are price changes for goods that are sold in their country of origin. International price fluctuations happen to goods that are exported and sold in other countries.

Often, price fluctuations follow the law of supply and demand. They may rise when there is a shortage or if a product is new. Prices fall when the market is flooded with a product or service, as companies compete for customers who have a wide range of choices. Many companies export goods to sell in other countries. These companies can make large profits if there's not already a similar product for sale on the local market and the demand is high. However, if the demand weakens, it may no longer be worthwhile to spend the money to ship a product overseas.

Both local and international price fluctuations can impact the nation's economy. Local fluctuations affect the ability of people to buy goods and services. They also affect the ability of business owners to make a profit. During recessions and depressions, people often cut back on buying things they don't really need. Businesses often lower prices to attract increasingly scarce buyers. Charging less may attract some customers, but it also reduces profits.

Price fluctuations also affect the job market. If fewer people are buying a company's products, prices fall and profits decrease, and the company may cut its workforce. Many companies severely cut production during the Great Depression. Unemployment rose because of these production cuts. By cutting production, companies saved money they would have otherwise spent on raw materials and labor. Yet, they also limited the number of their products available for sale to consumers. This further damaged their chances of profiting from their products.

Another factor that can help cause a depression is inflation. Inflation happens in two ways. Prices for most products can go up beyond what people are used to spending for them, or their

Falling demand for products like cars can affect the job security of a wide range of workers, from the people who build the cars and the people who sell them, to the people who make their parts and repair them.

money could drop in value (it is worth less and can buy less than before). Sometimes, both things occur together. In either case, people can no longer buy products for the same relatively low price they might have paid before. Stores and businesses

may have to close because people can no longer afford their increasingly expensive products or services.

Natural disasters and wars also play a role in the beginnings of depressions. Many of the depressions of the nineteenth century were caused by droughts or crop failures. Wars can help bring on depressions when fighting destroys factories, farmland, and materials. Countries at war may have to borrow money from other countries to pay for the expenses of continued fighting. Repaying the debt can severely stress a nation already battered by war. Yet, ironically, wars can also help end depressions by putting people to work making things like weapons, armored vehicles, aircraft, ships, and uniforms.

Events taking place in other parts of the world can also help cause recessions and depressions. During the 1920s, much of Europe was still recovering from World War I. Factories in many European countries had been damaged by the war, and these countries had to import goods from the United States in order to rebuild. The United States profited greatly from this trade imbalance at first. But when European

A German family is forced to live in an abandoned railroad car during the financial crisis that swept through Europe during the 1920s.

economies collapsed, American companies lost much of their export business.

The Beginning of the Great Depression

The 1920s were a booming time for the United States. While much of Europe was struggling to recover from World War I, the United States was experiencing tremendous economic growth. Jobs were plentiful, and high production made goods affordable to many people. Money became a sign of success, and business leaders were widely admired. Stocks soared in value as more Americans invested, hoping to get rich. Many people, even wealthy and savvy businessmen, made risky stock investments in hopes of making a large profit.

On October 24, 1929, the stock market crashed, and millions of people lost money. The day went down in history as "Black Thursday." For many people, this represents the beginning of the Great Depression. Yet, Black Thursday was not the end of the slide. Stocks kept dropping in value for the rest of the month as panicked investors tried to sell off their increasingly devalued shares.

At first, the market crash didn't directly affect many families. Most average Americans didn't own stocks. Many who did held on to them, hoping that the market would recover. Retail sales remained strong through the end of the year as people kept buying products. Many people thought that the downturn would end soon.

Though most Americans had not been affected yet, many felt uneasy after the crash. They wondered what had caused it, and many different theories and explanations were put forward. President Herbert Hoover, who had been elected in 1928, blamed the lingering aftereffects of World War I. He also criticized stock market speculators who had hoped to make quick profits selling their stock at high prices. Others blamed the government for allowing businesses to merge into monopolies. They also blamed the government for allowing banks and other lenders to expand and contract credit for profit. Still others felt that too much of the country's wealth was concentrated in the hands of just a few rich people.

The Depression Sets In

At first, it appeared the depression might end quickly. President Hoover acted to kick-start the economy by lowering taxes and

The "Black Thursday" stock market crash of October 1929 made newspaper headlines even before the day was over. Today, the crash is often considered the beginning of the Great Depression.

asking businesses to keep wages at pre-crash levels. Many businesses did so, and some even raised wages for their workers.

Keeping wages high didn't hold off a growing economic slowdown, however. Many businesses were forced to cut workers as they cut production. Since more people lost their jobs, fewer people had money to buy products. People who still had jobs stopped buying things, even though prices had started falling. They were afraid that they, too, would soon lose their jobs and wanted to save as much as possible in case of emergency. This was a complete reversal from spending patterns in the 1920s, when many Americans enthusiastically bought things on credit while the economy was good and jobs were secure.

Bank failures shook the country's confidence. Many banks began calling in loans. People didn't have the money to repay what they owed. When people who had money in savings accounts heard that their bank might be struggling, many panicked and took their money out all at once. If enough bank customers did this, there was a "run on the bank." Lines formed outside of banks, as panicked depositors tried to withdraw all of their savings. Banks often failed or closed and locked their doors until the panic subsided. Many banks failed, with 659 banks closing in 1929 alone.

People who had money in banks that failed saw their savings wiped out. This was a huge additional blow to people who had already lost their jobs or suddenly needed to repay loans. Banks became less willing to risk their financial well-being by loaning money to people. Companies that relied on short-term loans to pay workers could no longer do so. They also had no access to loans that would allow them to maintain equipment and facilities, expand operations, or develop new

Investors rush to withdraw their savings following the 1929 stock market crash. Mass withdrawals made the economy worse, as stocks fell further and banks ran short on cash.

products. Individual borrowers could no longer obtain cash to buy houses or other goods and services. Money stopped circulating in the economy and spending dried up, which forced companies to cut production and jobs even further.

Investments also slowed, draining even more money out of the economy and stifling business development. This was the case, even though the stock market had rebounded to early 1929 levels by the spring of 1930. Gross investment in the United States had fallen by 35 percent between 1929 and 1930. Investment had almost slowed to a trickle by 1931. That year, $800 million was invested, down from $16.2 billion in 1929.

These drops in spending and investing made an already bad situation even worse. Business leaders saw their unsold products sitting on shelves and cut production further. As more people lost their jobs, demand for products fell even more. Many businesses took steps to prepare for the worst. They continued to cut production and prices, and stopped buying materials from other businesses. These were logical steps for them to take in order to survive. Yet, when thousands of businesses took these steps at the same time, it gravely weakened the economy.

MYTHS and FACTS

MYTH A depression is a normal part of the business cycle.

FACT While recessions are part of the normal business cycle, depressions are extremely severe economic downturns that take years for the economy to overcome and recover from.

MYTH The stock market crash of 1929 caused the Great Depression.

FACT While the stock market set off a panic, the economy was already struggling when the market crashed.

MYTH A depression in one country won't affect the rest of the world.

FACT Global economies are closely linked through international trade, and serious problems in one country can often set off trouble around the world.

CHAPTER THREE
GROWTH OF DEPRESSIONS

Depressions occur when recessions become particularly severe or last for a very long time. Recessions are part of the normal business cycle. Countries tend to climb out of them within a matter of months as production increases, companies begin hiring again, and people start spending money. In a depression, however, the downturn is steeper and more prolonged.

During a depression, economic indicators show that the economy is contracting. This means that the economy is continuing to get worse. Manufacturers produce less, businesses earn less, people spend less, and more workers become and remain unemployed. While these factors are also true of a recession, they either continue for a much longer period of time or are much worse during a depression.

The Great Depression Deepens

Even as the depression deepened in 1930, the situation didn't seem any worse to some Americans than it had been during the last recession. Just before the economic boom of the 1920s began, the country had suffered through a recession that lasted from 1920 to 1921. Unemployment had averaged 11.9 percent during that time. By the end of 1930, the unemployment rate had not reached 9 percent yet. The Great Depression would not fully set in until 1931, when it became a global problem.

In the fall of 1930, President Hoover formed a committee called the President's Committee for Employment in an attempt to end the crisis. The organization did very little to help the situation. It failed to gather any real statistics on the economic crisis or organize any relief efforts. Instead, it focused mostly on trying to restore the public's confidence in the economy. President Hoover and his government opposed federal relief efforts. They thought that people without jobs could still somehow get by without relief and government assistance.

With the federal government checked out, local and state governments were left to pick up the slack and deal with the needs of the growing number of unemployed people. By 1932, these governments had run out of funds. Raising state taxes was not an option, since many citizens would be unwilling and unable to pay. Some states issued bonds for sale in an effort to raise money, but few people were willing to buy them. (Bonds are certificates that governments sell to citizens to help fund public projects. Someone who buys a bond is promised a profit on his or her investment after a certain period of time has passed.) Many states also had laws forbidding their governments to operate with unbalanced budgets (meaning that they couldn't spend more than they took in). In 1932, only eight states offered any sort of relief payments to unemployed workers.

The presidency of Herbert Hoover *(right)* was marred by the Great Depression, which steadily grew worse during his single term in office.

The Gold Standard and a Balanced Budget

When the Great Depression first began in 1929, the value of the U.S. dollar was directly linked to the value of gold. This "gold standard" meant that people could take their paper money or bonds into a bank and have it redeemed for an equivalent amount of actual gold. Many of the world's economies at the time were based on the gold standard. The value of gold linked these economies together.

One problem with the gold standard was that it made the money supply very rigid. If governments printed money beyond the value of the gold held in banks, the money would lose value because it couldn't all be redeemed for gold. If people started to hoard money during these times when it became less valuable, waiting for its value to increase again, there would be a physical shortage of cash available. The gold standard also linked world economies closely together based on the global value of gold. Cash shortages in one country could affect the value of gold worldwide. Likewise, the number of people trading in their cash for gold would also affect its value.

After a wave of bank failures in some parts of Europe, problems soon spread to Great Britain, as worried people pulled their money out of British banks. The British pound was one of the most important currencies in the world and was linked to the value of many other currencies around the world. But people afraid of a bank collapse sought the safety of actual, physical wealth (rather than paper currency) and withdrew their gold from banks in large numbers. As a result, the pound lost value, and Great Britain was forced to stop using the gold standard in September 1931. From then on, British bank customers were not able to exchange paper currency for the equivalent amount of gold.

When Great Britain went off the gold standard, many other countries were also forced to abandon it. In the United States, however, the country's Federal Reserve (a federal agency that acts as the country's central bank) moved to keep the gold standard. The Federal Reserve had to cut the money supply—the amount of money in circulation. This was necessary because the amount of money in circulation (currency) had to equal the amount of U.S. gold reserves in banks. At this time, there was more currency in circulation than there

The Great Depression led many countries to stop basing the value of their currency on the value of gold, though people still invest in it as a more stable alternative to the volatile stock market.

was gold to back it. Siphoning this excess currency out of circulation meant raising interest rates on loans. This made it more expensive for people to borrow money, so soon less money was in circulation. This led to deflation—scarcity of cash, decreased purchasing, a wholesale drop in prices, and a drop in production.

Banks called in loans, and customers postponed buying things until they had more cash and in the hope of even lower prices ahead. Yet, the fall in production led to layoffs and higher unemployment and even less spending. In many cases, banks had to foreclose on homes because people couldn't pay their debts. Within the next two years, more than half a million mortgages would be foreclosed (which meant that people lost their homes). As news and rumors spread about banks struggling because of loans not being repaid, depositors began to withdraw their money, fearing that their savings would be lost if the bank failed. This led to even more bank collapses. More than five hundred U.S. banks failed in just the first month after Britain went off the gold standard. By the end of 1931, there had been 2,293 bank failures in the United States.

Meanwhile, unemployment continued to rise. By the end of 1931, unemployment in the United States had risen to 15.9 percent. The country faced economic problems far worse than anything it had ever faced before. Tax receipts for the federal government fell by $900 million, while expenses rose by $200 million. The federal budget went into a $500 million deficit. A deficit means that the government is spending more money than it is receiving in a given period of time, such as a year.

Today, it is common for the government to continue spending money, even when there is a budget deficit. But at the time

A sign in New York City keeps track of the growing national debt, which at that point totaled more than $10 trillion. Unlike during the Depression years, the government is no longer reluctant to spend more money than it earns.

of the Great Depression, balancing the budget seemed like an important first step in fixing the economy. In late 1931, Hoover asked Congress to pass a tax increase in order to balance the budget. The higher taxes placed an even greater burden on people who were out of work or still employed but struggling with lower wages and devalued currency.

Tariff Trouble

In the postwar years—after World War I but before the Great Depression—the United States had profited greatly from

The Dust Bowl

A severe drought struck parts of the Midwestern and Great Plains states in 1930 and lasted until 1936 in many parts of the region. Farmers who had already been struggling with low crop prices saw their crops wither and their soil turn to dust and blow away. Much of the region's topsoil had been weakened

Droughts and dust storms that swept across the Great Plains states during the early 1930s wiped out the livelihoods of many farmers and contributed to the Great Depression.

by poor farming practices over several decades. High prairie winds would come and blow the topsoil away. At times, the clouds of dust blackened the sky.

Millions of acres of farmland were rendered useless by the drought. Hundreds of thousands of people, sometimes called Okies because many came from hard-hit Oklahoma, were forced to leave their homes. Many ended up working for very low pay picking fruit and other crops on the West Coast. They often faced discrimination and rough treatment. Author John Steinbeck documented the plight of the Okies in his classic novel *The Grapes of Wrath*, while folk singer Woody Guthrie sang songs about the Dust Bowl on his album *Dust Bowl Ballads*.

selling goods to a war-ravaged Europe. At the same time, the U.S. government had imposed high tariffs on foreign goods. Tariffs are taxes on imports from other countries. They are meant to protect domestic businesses by making goods from overseas more expensive for people to buy.

In 1927, a world economic conference had ended with many governments agreeing to stop imposing tariffs on foreign goods. The idea was that world trade would improve if there were fewer tariffs and, as a result, the world economy would experience healthy growth.

Many business and government leaders in the United States, however, still supported tariffs. They felt that tariffs protected domestic companies by making their products more competitive. After the stock market crash of 1929, business leaders in the United States pushed the government to set another tariff, despite the 1927 agreement. The result was a tariff bill called the Smoot-Hawley Tariff, passed in 1930. Hoover had originally meant for the tariff to help protect farmers, but it had the opposite effect.

Other nations resented the new tariff. Many of these countries owed money to the United States and couldn't hope to pay their debts unless they could sell their products to American consumers. The United States was the biggest foreign market at that time. In retaliation, European countries passed their own tariff laws against the United States. As a consequence of the new global tariffs, world trade fell sharply. This made it harder for manufacturers, farmers, and others to sell their goods overseas and made the depression worse for people all around the world.

By 1933, the consumer price index (a statistic that measures average prices for goods) in the United States had dropped

Rows of foreign cars sit on a dock in Portland, Oregon. National economies are closely linked today, meaning that problems in one country's economy can affect the economies of nations all over the world.

18 percent from 1929 levels. Falling prices made it hard for businesses to keep their wages at the same level, as they had promised in 1929. Many of the country's largest corporations, such as U.S. Steel and Ford, started cutting wages in 1931. By the time Franklin Delano Roosevelt (known as FDR) took office as president in 1933, the country's GDP had fallen from $103.6 billion to $56.4 billion. Even with the extensive relief efforts that were part of FDR's New Deal program, it took the economy ten years to make up this lost ground in American productivity.

CHAPTER FOUR
EFFECTS
OF DEPRESSIONS

By their very definition, economic depressions linger for a long time. People who live through them often have vivid memories of trying to survive the long, lean years. They may remember family members losing their jobs or ending up jobless themselves. People who were children at the time may remember their parents worrying about buying food or paying the bills. Many survivors of severe economic depressions alter their spending patterns for decades after recovery, remaining extremely careful with their money for the rest of their lives.

In the short term, people often have to make serious sacrifices during a depression. Families cut their spending on all but the most necessary goods. Today, modern families would likely cut back on things like Internet connections, cable television, vacations, and clothes and toy shopping. They may drive less or get rid of their second car in order to save money on gas, repairs, and insurance. Families may also sell off their prized possessions like vacation homes, boats, jewelry, or family heirlooms to make ends meet. If a parent's wages or hours are cut or if a family member loses his or her job, younger members of the family may have to look for work to help the family get by.

Unemployment

Rising unemployment both contributes to a depression and indicates that an economic slump is taking place. A rising unemployment rate reveals that businesses are not only not hiring new workers but are in fact cutting their workforce.

The effects of rising unemployment can be far-reaching. A higher unemployment rate means that more workers are jobless and looking for employment. Without their paychecks, they have very little to spend. Even workers who still have their jobs contribute to the continued slump. They may save more of their money rather than spending it, fearful that they, too, will soon lose their jobs. During depressions, unemployment may reach into the double digits. During the Great Depression, unemployment peaked at around 25 percent in 1933, which means that one out of every four American workers was out of a job.

Falling Demand

Demand for products falls during depressions. People spend their money only on things that they really need and cut back on or eliminate unessential purchases. They may put off buying new clothes and instead repair their clothes, or change their eating habits by buying less expensive food. Big-ticket and luxury items are among the first to be cut out of budgets. Families put off buying new cars or appliances, such as refrigerators.

Steep discounts may be a good thing for consumers, but they are bad for business. Reduced profits on discounted goods may eventually result in lower production, layoffs, and more widespread economic decline.

With demand for their products falling, manufacturers are forced to cut production and jobs. This affects other industries as well. When business slows and cash gets tight, companies cut back on the purchasing of goods and services

from other businesses—for example, office equipment and supplies, manufacturing equipment, and accountants.

Bankruptcies

In a depression, creditors—institutions or individuals who loan money—often call in their debts in an effort to keep money moving in and out of the firm smoothly. They may also call in their loans if they hear that a business is in trouble and may be unable to pay. With business down, the debtor cannot afford to pay off all of his or her loans and may be forced to declare bankruptcy.

Bankruptcy is a legally declared inability of a person or organization to pay off creditors. Declaring bankruptcy is a way to assure creditors that their loans will be paid off. It gives the lender and debtor an opportunity to come up with a payment plan and realistic repayment schedule that will satisfy the lenders and give the debtors some extra time and breathing room. In a worst-case scenario, the person or business owner may have to sell off assets like real estate, office equipment, or even the business itself to pay off his or her debts.

A store is forced to sell off all of its inventory and close. Bankruptcy gives individuals and businesses an opportunity to work out arrangements for paying off their debts.

Not only businesses can declare bankruptcy. Individuals can, too, when they fall too far behind in their debts. Bankruptcy does not wipe away debt or free you from repaying it. It simply gives you more time to do so and may reduce the amount owed somewhat. The drawback is that you will be considered much less credit-worthy in the future and will probably have trouble obtaining loans, mortgages, and credit cards.

Shrinking Credit

Credit problems are another factor that can both signal the beginning of an economic slump and contribute further to the downturn. Before the Great Depression began, people had freely borrowed money in order to purchase homes and new and expensive technological wonders, such as automobiles, refrigerators, and radios. At the time, banks and other creditors had the fluidity to make these loans because cash was flowing freely throughout the expanding economy. But when the stock market collapsed and creditors started calling in loans, many people couldn't pay them back. Banks collapsed, and bankers became much less willing to risk lending money again for much of the rest of the depression years.

The restricted credit harmed the economy in several ways. People could no longer borrow money in order to purchase goods, nor could they borrow money to help pay off their other debts. Businesses also had a much harder time borrowing money. Businesses often rely on short-term loans in order to pay workers and buy supplies and materials. They use their product stock as a guarantee that they can pay the loan. For example, a store may use the value of its merchandise as a guarantee or proof that it can repay the loan it is asking for. But if businesses can't borrow money, they can't pay workers or purchase materials for the manufacture of their products, and business grinds to a halt. This tends to deepen the slump.

Closed banks became a common sight during the Great Depression. Banks across the country failed as people withdrew their savings and failed to pay off their debts.

Price Fluctuations

Prices for goods generally tend to drop during depressions. This sounds like good news, as it would make it easier for

people with little money to make purchases. However, it actually spells trouble for the economy. Sellers are forced to lower prices on their goods to attract buyers. They may have to drop prices to the point where they are forced to sell their products at a loss. If they keep losing money this way, businesses may eventually be forced to close.

Lower prices do not just apply to goods and services. They can also mean lower wages and lower values for homes. If workers receive lower wages, they do not have as much money to spend on goods and services. This can also hurt businesses further. Unfortunately, a price that does not drop is the amount of debt that a person owes on loans to banks or credit card companies. There's also the chance that some goods could actually go up in price, even during a depression. Shortages sometimes happen during depressions. Business owners who make or sell a product that's in high demand may take advantage of the situation by raising prices, especially if that product is considered essential, such as bread, eggs, meat, or fuel.

Social Upheaval

Depressions are often marked by social unrest, and sometimes major changes take place in society as a result. During these times, people feel frightened and insecure. They may be angry at the government for mishandling the economy or resent the wealthy who don't share their hardships. People hungry for change may switch political parties and take their anger out on politicians by voting them out of office.

During the Great Depression, angry voters blamed President Herbert Hoover, a member of the Republican Party, for the country's economic problems. They also blamed Republican members of Congress. Republicans had controlled both the presidency and Congress all through the 1920s. Republicans lost control of both the House and the Senate in the midterm election of 1930. In 1932, Hoover himself lost the presidential election in a landslide to Democrat Franklin Delano Roosevelt.

Other public demonstrations of dissatisfaction are not as peaceful, orderly, and civic-minded as voting. In past depressions, riots have been common responses to foreclosures and shortages. Sometimes, mobs stormed and occupied public buildings to protest government policies. The unemployed may march in demonstrations. In the past, demonstrators have clashed with police and even the military during depressions, sometimes resulting in death and injury.

Bonnie Parker and Clyde Barrow were among the most famous of the bank robbers whose exploits captivated many Americans during the Great Depression.

Crime may also rise during depressions. Desperate people may go outside of the law in order to make money or obtain food, robbing banks, committing burglaries, or shoplifting. Violent crimes like murders may also increase. During the Great Depression, for example, bank robbers like John Dillinger and the famous duo of Bonnie Parker and Clyde Barrow captured the public's imagination by robbing the banks that some people blamed for causing the depression and seizing their homes, farms, or savings. These violent criminals were almost beloved figures, mistakenly regarded by many struggling and angry Americans as modern-day Robin Hoods, stealing from the rich and giving to the poor.

The Bonus Army

One of the largest demonstrations to take place during the Great Depression was a June 1932 march on Washington, D.C., by about twenty thousand World War I veterans. They marched to ask the government to pay them bonuses that had been promised to them for their service. The bonuses were not supposed to come due until 1945, but many of the veterans needed the money immediately to survive the depression. The Senate refused to allow the early payments.

Many of the veterans left, but about four thousand stayed behind and rioted on July 28. Soldiers were called in to drive them out and destroy their camp using tanks and tear gas. The group finally left after Congress appropriated $100,000 to send them home. Congress eventually voted to allow cash payments of the bonuses in 1936.

Life During the Great Depression

Life for many Americans changed drastically during the Great Depression. Many were out of work and struggled to buy food and other necessities. Many people had a hard time finding enough to eat. One study conducted at the time found that families with at least one fully employed member had 66 percent less illness than families in which no one was working. Some people living in rural areas sometimes ate weeds to survive. People living in cities sometimes had to dig through garbage cans and city dumps for food.

As unemployment grew, many men started traveling in search of work, sometimes hopping trains to cover greater distances. By 1932, men dressed in battered clothing and seeking work were common sights in many cities and towns. Often, these wandering men were discriminated against by people who thought they were trying to take jobs from working people in the town. At worst, they were seen as potentially dangerous drifters or even classified by local laws as vagrants and subject to arrest and imprisonment. Settlements of unemployed men and impoverished, homeless families living in crude shacks—called "Hoovervilles" after President Hoover—cropped up at the edges of towns and cities. Getting almost no government help from the Hoover administration, charities in some cities and towns set up programs to attempt to feed the growing number of hungry and homeless people.

Many segments of society faced prejudice during the Great Depression. African Americans had faced heavy discrimination throughout the country long before the depression began. As the depression grew worse, working African Americans were often laid off from their jobs so that those jobs could be

Some people who lost their homes during the Great Depression ended up living in communities of crude shacks on the outskirts of towns and cities. They were often called "Hoovervilles" after the unpopular Depression-era president, Herbert Hoover.

given to white workers. About 50 percent of African American workers were unemployed by 1932, significantly more than whites. Other minority groups faced similar pressure. Mexican Americans living in large cities like Detroit, Michigan, or in

agricultural communities like California's San Joaquin Valley were sometimes seen as holding jobs that should go to whites. Programs were set up to persuade Mexican Americans to return to Mexico. Those who resisted were often threatened, intimidated, or beaten.

Poor whites also faced discrimination. Farmers who lost their land to foreclosure or who fled drought conditions during the Dust Bowl years were forced to wander in search of work. Many went to West Coast states like California or Oregon in search of agricultural work. Those that found work were often badly paid and poorly treated.

CHAPTER FIVE

COMING OUT OF A DEPRESSION

Though the United States has suffered through several depressions during its history, there is still no single formula for coming out of a depression. Depressions are caused by a number of different events that take place at the same time. Recoveries from them are equally dependent upon a number of different factors coming together at the same time.

Relief Programs and Policy Initiatives

One important step in helping the economy recover is to set relief programs in place to help those in need. Relief programs may be relatively simple programs that distribute food or clothing to people in need. They may also be complex employment programs designed to find jobs for people who need work.

To bring the economy out of a slump, the government often makes policy changes designed to help businesses increase productivity and hire workers. The Federal Reserve

System, which serves as a central bank, often lowers interest rates during a slump. The lower interest rates encourage borrowing and make it easier for individuals and businesses to repay lenders.

President Hoover and Congress raised taxes during the Great Depression, a move that many economists today feel made the crisis worse. The usual government response during economic slowdowns is to lower taxes. Lowering taxes lessens the tax burden on people and businesses. Money that they would ordinarily have spent on taxes can then be spent in other ways. Consumers can buy products, while businesses can increase production. This spending stimulates the economy and helps it climb out of the trough.

In early 2008, the federal government mailed out rebate checks to taxpayers in an attempt to jump-start the economy. Instead, the economy worsened.

Tax refunds are another tool the government uses to encourage spending. With refunds, taxpayers are given a check from the Internal Revenue Service for a fixed amount. When the housing bubble burst in 2007, the government responded by issuing tax refunds to everyone who filled out tax forms for the year 2007. Even people who did not have

Women entered the workforce in large numbers after the United States entered World War II, especially in factories for making weapons and supplies for the war effort. The manufacturing boom pulled the country out of the depression.

to pay any taxes for the year could receive a refund so long as they filled out the form.

In order to keep people employed during an economic slump, the government may also bail out struggling businesses

that employ large numbers of workers. These bailouts, often used for large manufacturers like automakers, can come in the form of loans, grants, subsidies, or even management help. During the Great Depression, Herbert Hoover bailed out some investors. Similar action was taken in the fall of 2008, as the government approved a $700 billion package to help banks recover from bad mortgage loans.

Wars can help bring on depressions, just as the War of 1812 helped lead to the Panic of 1819. War reduces the number of workers available and often diverts production from retail goods to military supplies. When a war ends, economies may sink into recessions because there aren't enough job openings for the many thousands of soldiers returning to civilian life. The country may have spent vast sums of money on the war and now has to deal with serious debt. Factories and fields may have been wrecked by fighting, and large segments of the workforce may have died in fighting or fled to safety in other countries.

Ironically, war can also help bring a country out of a depression. The United States had come through the worst of the Great Depression by 1935, despite the recession of 1937. However, unemployment remained relatively high and production low until the United States became involved in World War II (1941–1945). Production leaped to all-time highs and unemployment dropped as factories went to work manufacturing supplies for the war effort. The economy continued to boom even after the war, as factories switched back from manufacturing military supplies to making consumer goods.

Depression Mentality

The years of hardship made a profound, even traumatic, impression on many Americans who lived through the Great Depression. Some had seen their homes taken away. Others had taken any work they could find, no matter how back-breaking, to put food on the table. Their experiences gave rise to an attitude toward money sometimes called a depression mentality.

This mind-set is marked by extreme caution with spending and high concern about financial security. Many people who lived through the Great Depression were ever afterward frugal (low-spending), unwilling to take on debt, and careful to save money for the future and in case of emergencies. During economic boom times, a depression mentality can seem overly cautious amid prosperity and bountiful financial opportunities. When the economy falters, however, people rediscover the importance of saving money and the wisdom of handling it safely and responsibly.

The New Deal and the End of the Great Depression

President Franklin Roosevelt faced a daunting task when he took office in 1933. The nation's economy was in ruins. People across the country were disheartened. During his inauguration speech, Roosevelt sought to reassure the country by announcing that "the only thing we have to fear is fear itself."

Roosevelt immediately set to work to reassure the nation by beginning work on the New Deal. The massive New Deal program was a series of federal programs and agencies designed to counteract the effects of the depression. One of the goals of the

President Franklin D. Roosevelt led the United States out of the Great Depression and through World War II. As testament to his popularity among grateful and still-shaken Depression-era Americans, he was the only president ever elected to four terms.

New Deal was to lower production of crops and products to meet the low demand of consumers. Another goal was to increase consumer demand in part by supplying jobs for people in public works fields and getting cash back into their hands. With

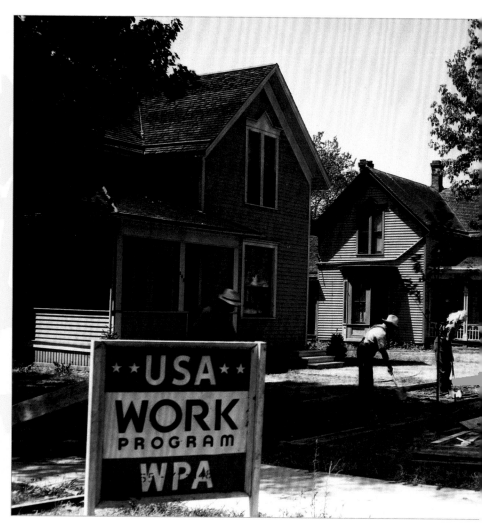

Public works programs put millions of unemployed Americans back to work during the 1930s. These men are repairing a sidewalk as part of one such program.

people earning money by building roads, dams, and schools, they once again had money to spend on goods and services.

One of Roosevelt's first actions was to get Congress to pass a nationwide bank holiday. On this day, all of

the country's banks would be closed and people would not be able to withdraw money. Congress also passed the Emergency Banking Act, a law calling for the government to inspect banks. Another law called the Glass-Steagall Act set tougher rules for banks. It also provided insurance to depositors through a new agency called the Federal Deposit Insurance Corporation (FDIC). Even today, this agency guarantees that people will not lose all of their money in the event of a bank collapse.

Other programs provided direct assistance to people in need. Several bills were passed to help farmers and homeowners pay their mortgages. The Federal Emergency Relief Agency provided grants to states that helped more than twenty million people through public works projects that gave them jobs and improved the quality of their lives. The Fair Standards of Labor Act limited the number of hours that most laborers could work and set the country's first minimum wage. The Social Security Act of 1935 included three major programs: a fund for retired workers, unemployment insurance for people who lose their jobs, and welfare grants for the poor.

Broader New Deal efforts included the Agricultural Adjustment Act, a law designed to raise farm prices. The National Industrial Recovery Act provided for an expanded national public works effort overseen by the Public Works Administration. It also included new guidelines to guarantee fair and competitive business practices.

While the New Deal did not end the Great Depression, it greatly lessened its severity. More people had jobs, and federal programs were put into place to help those unable to work. The New Deal programs also helped set up important government controls over the economy that helped the country better weather later recessions.

CHAPTER SIX

CAN A DEPRESSION HAPPEN AGAIN?

From 2003 to 2006, some sectors of the U.S. economy grew rapidly. Low interest rates and high-risk lending practices made it easy for people to borrow money. The housing market, in particular, soared as home prices rose and people kept building new houses.

However, the economy began slowing in late 2006. Home sales dropped, and so did new home construction. People who had built the new homes and businesses that had supplied building materials soon found that they had much less work than before. Despite the slump, the stock market kept rising, hitting an all-time high that year.

Yet, even the markets eventually dropped as bad news started coming in. Creditors lost money as people defaulted on their loans. In August 2008, unemployment rose to a five-year high of 6.1 percent, and credit tightened again. Some banks were even taken to the brink of collapse and were bought out by other banks. The government took steps to

Investors found reason to despair as the stock market plummeted during the fall of 2008. The collapse of several large financial firms spurred the steep decline.

bail out mortgage lenders Fannie Mae and Freddie Mac, as well as insurance giant AIG. In September 2008, the government even passed a $700 billion rescue plan to help struggling banks.

Placing Blame and Finding Reasons to Hope

In the fall of 2008, many economists predicted that the economy could fall into a severe recession or even a depression. Some economists felt the regulations that were put in place during the Great Depression had been seriously weakened over time and, as a result, the FDIC might not be able to guarantee deposits in the event of a full-scale banking collapse. They pointed out that deregulating the activities of banks and lenders had brought on the credit crises by undoing some of these economic controls.

Other economists dismissed the idea. During the Great Depression, new policies were put into action governing the way that banks do business and guaranteeing that money held by the banks would be insured. Economists felt that these safeguards—along with a broader government relief system than any that existed when the Great Depression began—would protect the economy in this latest crisis. Unlike when Herbert Hoover was in office, the government now willingly spends itself into a deficit in order to spur the economy and protect its citizens. Also, governments today are more ready to step in and offer direct aid to individuals and businesses during an economic crisis. In fact, in late 2008, President-elect Barack Obama proposed an economic stimulus and rescue package that involved public works

In the fall of 2008, the federal government began loaning money to struggling firms like American International Group, Inc. (AIG) in an attempt to stabilize the crumbling economy.

projects, homeowner and taxpayer relief, and assistance to banks, manufacturers, and small businesses. The cost of this large and ambitious plan was estimated to be as much as $1 trillion. In February 2009, President Obama signed this package into law.

Drawing Parallels

There are some similarities, however, in the circumstances that caused the Great Depression and the financial crisis of 2008. Banks and lending institutions, including some very old and respected firms, went under (failed) in 2008, just as they did in 1929. Unemployment rose dramatically and spending fell sharply in both eras. In both economic crises, the stock market fell dramatically and stocks lost much of their value.

Yet, these same kinds of events have occurred in several recessions since the Great Depression. During those recessions, economists would sometimes issue dire warnings of coming depressions. Instead, the economy recovered after a period of months or even years. While conditions were bad during these times, they never resulted in a depression.

Given the effective protections and safeguards put into the economy during the Great Depression, chances are good that the economic crisis of 2008 will be viewed in future years as a strong and serious recession, but one that the nation actively pulled itself out of, thereby avoiding another depression.

GLOSSARY

bankruptcy A legal process intended to ensure equality among the creditors of a corporation or individual declared to be bankrupt, or a person or corporation's inability to discharge all debts as they come due.

bond A certificate of ownership of a specified portion of a debt due to be paid by a government or corporation to an individual holder and usually bearing a fixed rate of interest.

corporation An organized body, especially a business, that has been granted a state charter recognizing it as a separate legal entity having its own rights, privileges, and liabilities distinct from those of the individuals within the entity.

credit Confidence in a purchaser's ability and intention to pay, displayed by entrusting the buyer with goods or services without immediate payment.

currency Something that is used as a medium of exchange; money.

debt Something that is owed or that one is bound to pay to or perform for another.

deficit The amount by which costs or debts exceed income or assets.

deflation A fall in the general price level or a contraction of credit and available money.

depression A period during which business, employment, and stock market values decline severely or remain at a very low level of activity.

economy A network of producers, distributors, and consumers of goods and services in a local, regional, national, or global community.

gross domestic product (GDP) The total market value of goods and services produced by workers and capital within a nation's borders during a given period.

gross national product (GNP) The total monetary value of all final goods and services produced in a country during one year.

interest A sum paid or charged for the use of money or for borrowing money, often expressed as a percentage of money borrowed and to be paid back within a given time.

production The process of producing goods that have exchange value.

profit The monetary surplus left to a producer or employer after deducting wages, rent, cost of raw materials, etc.

recession A period of general economic decline, defined usually as a contraction in the GDP for six months or longer. Marked by high unemployment, stagnant wages, and falling retail sales, a recession generally does not last longer than one year and is much milder than a depression.

stock Ownership shares of a particular company or corporation.

tariff A government tax on imports or exports.

FOR MORE INFORMATION

Board of Governors of the Federal Reserve System
20th Street and Constitution Avenue NW
Washington, DC 20551
Web site: http://www.federalreserve.gov
The Federal Reserve System serves as the nation's central
    bank. It consists of a seven-member Board of Governors
    with headquarters in Washington, D.C., and twelve
    Reserve Banks located in major U.S. cities.

Department of Finance Canada
Minister of Finance
140 O'Connor Street
Ottawa, ON K1A0G5
Canada
(613) 992-1573
Web site: http://www.fin.gc.ca
The Department of Finance Canada oversees the Canadian
    government's budget and spending.

Federal Deposit Insurance Corporation (FDIC)
Public Information Center
3501 North Fairfax Drive
Arlington, VA 22226

(877) 275-3342
Web site: http://www.fdic.gov
This is a government agency that insures bank deposits.

Government Finance Officers Association (GFOA)
1301 Pennsylvania Avenue NW, Suite 309
Washington, DC 20004
(202) 393-8020
Web site: http://www.gfoa.org
The GFOA works to enhance professionalism in public
    financial management in the United States and Canada.

National Council on Economic Education
1140 Avenue of the Americas
New York, NY 10036
(800) 338-1192
Web site: http://www.ncee.net
This is a group dedicated to expanding economic education
    in schools.

Treasury Board of Canada Secretariat
Strategic Communications and Ministerial Affairs
L'Esplanade Laurier, 9th Floor, East Tower
140 O'Connor Street
Ottawa, ON K1A 0R5
Canada
(877) 636-0656
Web site: http://www.tbs-sct.gc.ca
This is a government body that provides oversight of financial
    management functions in other departments and agencies.

U.S. Department of the Treasury
1500 Pennsylvania Avenue, NW
Washington, DC 20220
(202) 622-2000
Web site: http://www.ustreas.gov
The Department of the Treasury serves the American people
   and strengthens national security by managing the U.S.
   government's finances effectively, promoting economic
   growth and stability, and ensuring the safety, soundness,
   and security of the U.S. and international financial systems.

The World Bank
1818 H Street NW
Washington, DC 20433
(202) 473-1000
Web site: http://web.worldbank.org
This is a global network of economies designed to provide
   development assistance to other countries.

Web Sites

Due to the changing nature of Internet links, Rosen Publishing
has developed an online list of Web sites related to the subject
of this book. This site is updated regularly. Please use this link
to access the list:

http://www.rosenlinks.com/rwe/depr

FOR FURTHER READING

Badhan-Quallen, Sudipta. *Franklin Delano Roosevelt: A National Hero*. New York, NY: Sterling Publishing Company, 2007.

Cooper, Michael L. *Dust to Eat: Drought and Depression in the 1930s*. New York, NY: Clarion Books, 2004.

Downing, David. *Political and Economic Systems: Capitalism*. Chicago, IL: Heinemann, 2008.

Gilman, Laura Anne. *Economics*. Minneapolis, MN: Lerner Publications, 2006.

Landau, Elaine. *The Great Depression*. New York, NY: Children's Press, 2006.

Nardo, Don. *American History by Decade: The 1930s*. Farmington Hills, MI: Kidhaven Press, 2004.

Stein, R. Conrad. *The New Deal: Pulling America Out of the Great Depression*. Berkeley Heights, NJ: Enslow Publishers, Inc., 2006.

BIBLIOGRAPHY

Bonner, Bill, and Addison Wiggin. *Empire of Debt: The Rise of an Epic Financial Crisis*. Hoboken, NJ: John Wiley & Sons, Inc., 2006.

Cameron, Rondo. *A Concise Economic History of the World: From Paleolithic Times to the Present*. 3rd ed. New York, NY: Oxford University Press, 1997.

Flynn, Sean Masaki. *Economics for Dummies*. Hoboken, NJ: John Wiley & Sons, Inc., 2005.

Galbraith, John Kenneth. *The Great Crash: 1929*. Boston, MA: Houghton Mifflin Company, 1988.

Gordon, John Steele. *An Empire of Wealth: The Epic History of American Economic Power*. New York, NY: HarperCollins Publishers, 2004.

Gottheil, Fred. *Principles of Economics*. 4th ed. Mason, OH: Thomson Publishing, 2005.

Krugman, Paul. *The Return of Depression Economics*. New York, NY: W. W. Norton & Company, 1999.

Lanigan, Jane, ed. *Economics: Economic History*. Vol. 6. Danbury, CN: Grolier Educational, 2000.

Lanigan, Jane, ed. *Economics: Economic Theory*. Vol. 5. Danbury, CN: Grolier Educational, 2000.

Lawson, Alan. *A Commonwealth of Hope: The New Deal Response to Crisis*. Baltimore, MD: The Johns Hopkins University Press, 2006.

Lowenstein, Roger. *Origins of the Crash: The Great Bubble and Its Undoing*. New York, NY: The Penguin Press, 2004.

McElvaine, Robert S. *The Great Depression: America, 1929–1941*. New York, NY: Times Books, 1993.

Nardo, Don, ed. *The Great Depression*. San Diego, CA: Greenhaven Press, Inc., 2000.

Rauchway, Eric. *The Great Depression and the New Deal: A Very Short Introduction*. New York, NY: Oxford University Press, 2008.

Sowell, Thomas. *Basic Economics: A Citizen's Guide to the Economy*. New York, NY: Basic Books, 2000.

Steeples, Douglas, and David O. Whitten. *Democracy in Desperation: The Depression of 1893*. Westport, CN: Greenwood Press, 1998.

INDEX

About the Author

Jason Porterfield has authored numerous books for Rosen Publishing, including ones on economic topics. He earned his B.A. in history, English, and religion from Oberlin College in 2001, and holds an M.A. in journalism from Columbia College, Chicago. Porterfield lives in Chicago.

Photo Credits

Cover (top) © www.istockphoto.com/Andrey Prokhorov; cover (middle) © www.istockphoto.com/Lilli Day; cover (bottom) © Spencer Platt/Getty Images; pp. 1, 66 © Mario Tama/Getty Images; pp. 8–9 © Gail Mooney/Corbis; pp. 10–11 © Joel Stettenhein/Corbis; p. 14 © Joe Raedle/Getty Images; pp. 17, 33, 48–49 Library of Congress Prints and Photographs Division; pp. 22–23 © Justin Sullivan/Getty Images; p. 24 © Three Lions/Getty Images; p. 26 © FPG/Getty Images; p. 28 © MPI/Getty Images; p. 35 © Hybg Yeon-Je/AFP/Getty Images; pp. 37, 40, 58–59 © AP Photos; p. 38 © Arthur Rothstein/Resettlement Admininstration/Time & Life Pictures/Getty Images; pp. 44–45 © Emmanuel Dunard/AFP/Getty Images; p. 46 © Jim Watson/AFP/Getty Images; p. 51 © Hulton Archives/Getty Images; pp. 54–55 © American Stock/Getty Images; p. 57 © Jeff Fusco/Getty Images; p. 61 Keystone/Getty Images; pp. 62–63 © Minnesota Historical Society/Corbis; pp. 68-69 © Spencer Platt/Getty Images.

Designer: Sam Zavieh; Photo Researcher: Marty Levick